BUILD YOUR OWN DINOSAURS!
Mighty Moving Models!

Copyright © 2023 Hungry Tomato Ltd

First published in 2023 by Hungry Tomato Ltd
F15, Old Bakery Studios, Blewetts Wharf, Malpas Road, Truro, Cornwall,
TR1 1QH, UK.

A CIP catalogue record for this book is available from the British Library.

ISBN 978-1-915461-79-7

Printed in China

Discover more at
www.hungrytomato.com

CONTENTS

INTRODUCTION

Try your hand at building wonderful mighty moving models! Using smart and simple engineering principles you can make a whole collection of amazing prehistoric creatures that can nod, bend, race, and more! Don't miss the fun facts about the amazing prehistoric beasts in each project.

THIS BOOK IS INTERACTIVE!

Some of the projects in this book come with templates to help you cut pieces to the right shape and size. Use a smartphone to scan the QR code at the beginning of the project, to access a downloadable template that you can print out.

You will find QR codes at the end of some projects too. These will direct you to videos of the moving dinosaur models in action!

You can also find all templates and videos at:
https://www.hungrytomato.com/mighty-moving-models

TOP TIPS

- Before you start on any project, read the step-by-steps all the way through to get an idea of what you are aiming for. The pictures show what the steps tell you to do.

- Use a cutting mat, or similar surface, for cutting lengths of craft sticks, skewers, and anything else you may need.

- Use the sharp end of a pencil to make small holes in cardboard (see page 6 for method) or ask an adult to help, using either scissors or a craft knife.

- Use a pair of pliers to help straighten out and shape paper clips.

- Where strong glue is required, you may want to use a hot glue gun. Make sure you ask permission, and do not use it without an adult present. Strong liquid glue, such as wood or epoxy glue, will work well too.

EASY

MEDIUM

HARDER

These icons are a guide to the difficulty level of each project. They show you when you may need another pair of hands. You will find these icons at the top of the page, near the title of each project.

SAFETY FIRST

Be careful and use good sense when making these models. They are easy to understand but will require some cutting, drilling, gluing, and other awkward tasks that you may need some help with from an adult.

Watch out for this sign throughout the book. You may need help from an adult when completing these tasks.

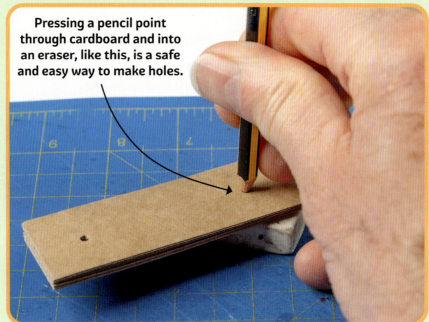

Pressing a pencil point through cardboard and into an eraser, like this, is a safe and easy way to make holes.

DISCLAIMER

The author, publisher, and bookseller cannot take responsibility for your safety. When you make and try out the projects, you do so at your own risk. Look out for the safety warning symbol (shown above) given throughout the book and call on adult assistance when you are cutting materials or using a craft knife, pair of pliers, drill, or hot glue.

TOOL KIT

Every project includes a list of everything you will need to build it. Most of the items you will need can be found around your home, or are readily available or inexpensive to buy from your local hardware or general-purpose store, or online.

TOOLS:

- Pair of compasses
- Pencil and pens
- Ruler
- Craft knife

- Strong glue
- School glue (PVA)
- Craft drill
- Pair of needle-nose pliers

- Wire cutters
- Pair of scissors
- Rubber
- Chopstick (or similar)

- Cutting mat
- Craft stick
- Screwdriver

DIPPING DRYOSAURUS

(dry-oh-SORE-us)

Dryosaurus had stiff tails that helped them with their balance, allowing them to run on two feet at high speeds without falling over.

WHAT YOU NEED:

- Air-dry clay
- 3 regular paper clips (about 25 mm/1 inch)
- 1 jumbo paper clip (about 50 mm/2 inches long)
- Craft cork
- 4 (6mm/1/4 inch) glass beads

TOOLS:

- Craft stick
- Pair of needle-nose pliers
- Strong glue
- Wire cutters
- Craft drill
- Pair of scissors

1 Shape the dinosaur body from air-dry clay. Press in the sides where the tops of the legs will fit, using the end of a craft stick. Repeat on the other side.

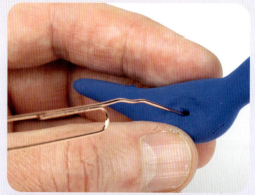

2 Make a hole right through the body with a straightened-out paper clip.

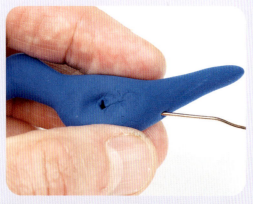

3 Make another hole under the tail for the linkage loop to fit into later.

4 Make some eyes from air-dry clay and press them into each side of the head. Form a mouth.

5 Make two legs, one for each side.

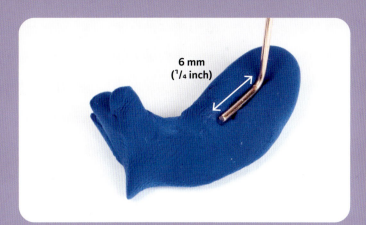

6 Using a paper clip, make a dent in the inner side of each leg, about 6 mm (¼ inch) long. The hip wire will mount into this groove.

7 Finish off the body by adding a pair of forearms. Set the dinosaur parts aside until they are set hard.

8 Use a drill to make a hole through the middle of the cork. Keep it as straight as possible.

9 Once the dinosaur has completely dried, thread a length of regular paper clip through the holes in the body. Fold over on both sides as shown and cut with wire cutters so the lengths are 6 mm (¼ inch).

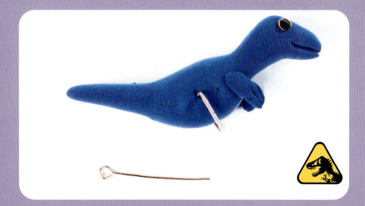

10 Straighten out a regular paper clip and, using pliers, bend a small loop in one end. Cut it to fit in the hole under the tail.

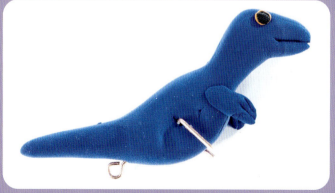

11 Push the wire into the hole under the tail and secure it with a dab of glue.

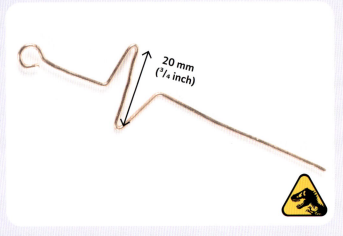

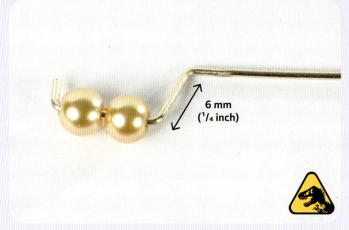

12 Fold the remaining regular paper clip in a zigzag shape as shown, and bend a loop at the end.

20 mm (³/₄ inch)

13 Fold the jumbo paper clip as shown and thread on two glass beads.

6 mm (¹/₄ inch)

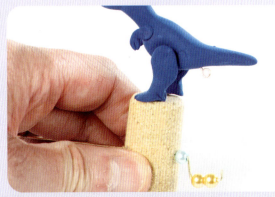

14 Glue the grooves in the legs to the hip wires. Glue the feet to the top of the cork. Thread another bead onto the long part of what will be the crank wire, and push it through the cork.

15 Thread the final bead onto the other side of the crank wire, then fold the wire into a handle.

The zigzag in the wire allows you to adjust the length of the pushrod, so that you can get the movement you want.

16 Turn the crank so that the beads are at their highest. Bend the body over so that the dinosaur's head is at its lowest. Fold another loop into the other end of the zigzag wire, so that it lines up with the tail loop and the crank.

SCAN HERE TO SEE ME IN ACTION!

17 Fit the zigzag wire into place, between the beads and under the tail.

TURN THE HANDLE TO MAKE THE DRYOSAURUS ROCK BACK AND FORTH!

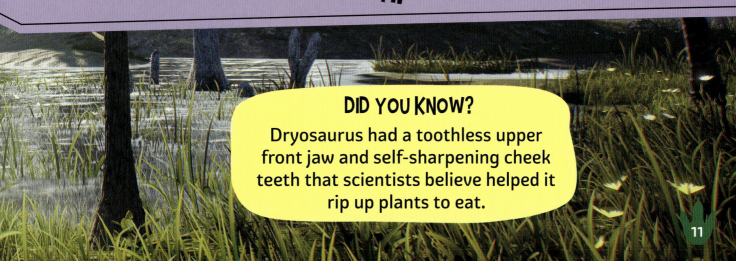

DID YOU KNOW?

Dryosaurus had a toothless upper front jaw and self-sharpening cheek teeth that scientists believe helped it rip up plants to eat.

BENDING BRACHIOSAURUS
(BRAK-ee-oh-sore-us)

Use the QR code to access the template you need.

WHAT YOU NEED:
- Assorted craft card
- Felt-tip pens
- Regular paper clip (about 25 mm/1 inch)
- Wooden clothes peg
- Plastic eyes

TOOLS:
- Pair of scissors
- Pair of needle-nose pliers
- Wire cutters
- School glue (PVA)
- Chopstick (or similar)
- Craft drill

Brachiosaurus were massive dinosaurs. They could have weighed as much as four African elephants!

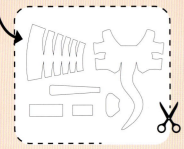

1 Copy or trace the shapes from the template onto thin craft card and cut them out. Decorate with felt-tip pens.

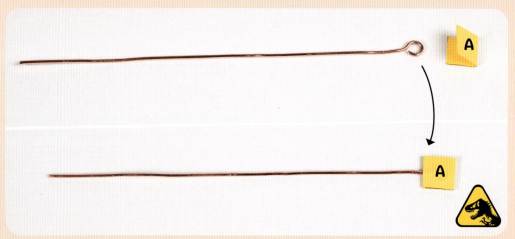

2 Straighten out the paper clip. Add a loop to the end, using a pair of pliers. Fold piece A in half so that it will sandwich the loop on the paper clip. Glue it into place.

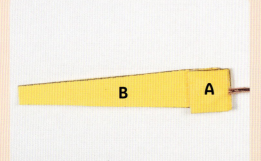

3 Glue the covered loop to the wide end of the pull tab (B).

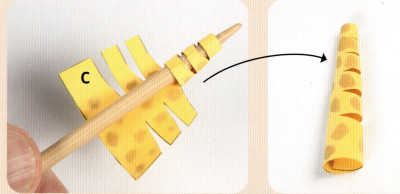

4 Roll each section of the neck (C) around and glue them together. A chopstick works as a useful tool for shaping this piece.

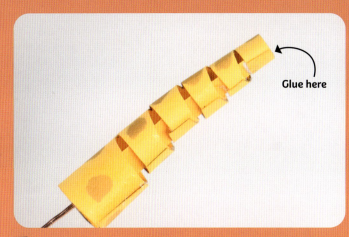

5 Thread the long pull tab up through the neck and glue to the inside of the top section, at the front.

Glue here

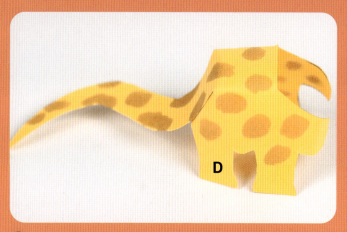

6 Fold the body (D) into shape and glue the edges together.

D

E

7 Glue the head (E) into place, as shown.

8 Drill a hole right through the end of a clothes peg.

Glue on some plastic eyes!

9 Glue the neck inside the body.

10 Thread the wire down through the holes in the clothes peg, then glue the feet along the top edge of the clothes peg.

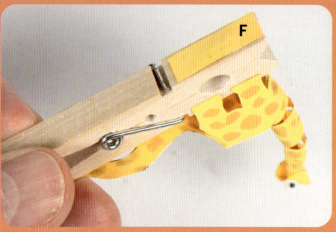

11 With the neck upright, bend over the wire and use wire cutters to snip off the excess, as shown.

12 Glue the rectangular piece of card (F) over the wire to secure it into position.

DID YOU KNOW?
Brachiosaurus had front legs that were longer than their back ones. This may have made it easier for them to reach the leaves on tall trees.

SQUEEZE THE CLOTHES PEG TO MAKE THE BRACHIOSAURUS REACH DOWN WITH ITS LONG NECK!

SCAN HERE
TO SEE ME IN ACTION!

PEEPING CAMARASAURUS
(KAM-ar-a-sore-us)

Use the QR code to access the template you need.

WHAT YOU NEED:
- Cardboard
- 2 paper split pins
- Craft card
- Felt-tip pens

TOOLS:
- Pair of scissors
- School glue (PVA)
- Pencil
- Ruler

These plant-eating dinosaurs probably lived and moved around in herds.

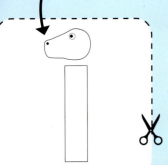

1 Copy or trace the shapes from the template onto bright craft card and then cut them out.

2 Cut two strips of cardboard measuring 30 x 150 mm (1¼ x 6 inches) and one strip measuring 30 x 125 mm (1¼ x 5 inches).

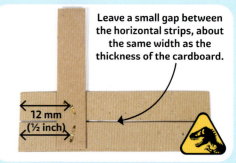

Leave a small gap between the horizontal strips, about the same width as the thickness of the cardboard.

12 mm (½ inch)

3 Join together the three strips using the two paper split pins, as shown. Use the point of a pencil to make the holes for the pins to go through (see page 6).

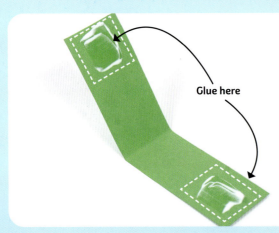

Glue here

4 Cut a strip of craft card long enough to wrap over both sides of the horizontal bars of cardboard. Add glue to the tips.

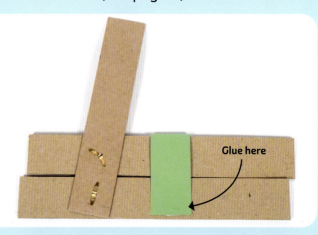

Glue here

5 Fold it around the cardboard and glue it to the lower cardboard bar on both sides, so the upper piece of cardboard can slide freely from side to side.

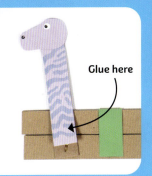

Glue here

6 Decorate your dinosaur's head and neck with felt-tip pens and then glue the pieces to the vertical cardboard bar.

Glue here

7 Cut out some bushes from craft card and glue them together to the lower bar, making sure that the upper bar and dinosaur can move freely.

SCAN HERE
TO SEE ME IN ACTION!

PUSH AND PULL THE UPPER BAR TO MAKE THE CAMARASAURUS PEEP OUT FROM THE BUSHES!

DID YOU KNOW?

The Camarasaurus had hollow chambers in its spine, which made the neck skeleton lighter.

RACING PACHYCEPHALOSAURUS

(pack-ee-SEF-al-oh-sore-us)

Use the QR code to access the template you need.

WHAT YOU NEED:

- Thin cardboard
- Felt-tip pens
- 3 jumbo paper clips (about 50 mm/2 inches long)
- Paper cup
- 6 (6mm/1/4 inch) glass beads

TOOLS:

- Pair of scissors
- Pair of needle-nose pliers
- School glue (PVA)
- Ruler
- Pencil
- Wire cutters

Get your Pachycephalosaurus racing with a simple turn of a handle. How fast can you make them run?

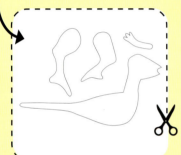

1 Copy or trace the shapes from the template onto thin cardboard and cut them out.

2 Use felt-tip pens to decorate the body pieces with suitable markings.

3 Spread a thin layer of glue onto the back of the body. Hold a straightened-out paper clip against it, as shown.

4 Glue the two halves of the body together, with the paper clip in between (it will be removed later).

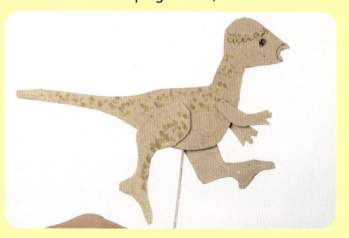

5 Glue the arms and legs onto both sides.

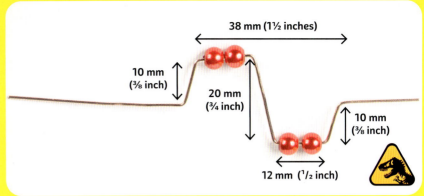

6 Make the second dinosaur in the same way. Once the glue is dry, pull out the paper clips.

7 To make a crank wire, straighten out a jumbo paper clip. Fold it into the shape shown above, using pliers and adding the beads as you do so.

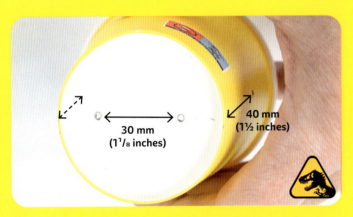

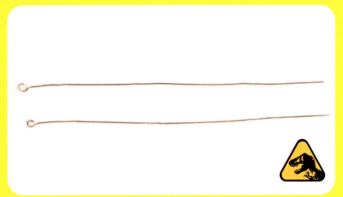

8 Use the point of a pencil to make holes in the bottom of the cup, as shown. Next, 40 mm (1½ inches) up from the base, make two holes on opposite sides of the cup that line up with the holes in the base.

9 Straighten out the two remaining jumbo paper clips. Bend a small loop into the end of each wire using the pliers.

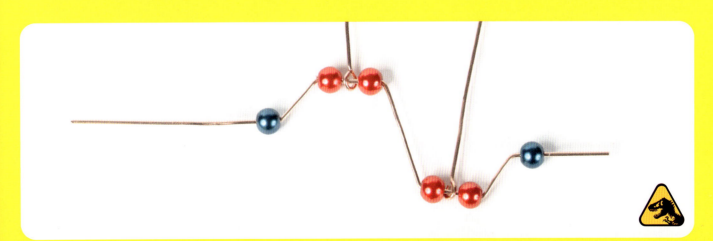

10 Thread the loops onto the crank wire between the two pairs of beads, and pinch closed, so they can't fall off. Thread the remaining beads onto each end of the wire.

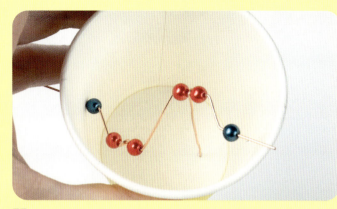

11 Thread the long wires through the holes in the bottom of the cup, then thread the crank wire into place through the side holes, long end first.

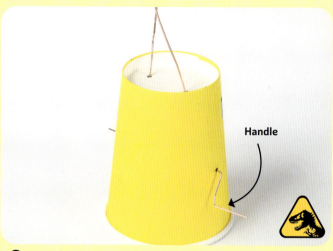

Handle

12 Fold a handle into the long end of the crank wire. Cut the upright wires with wire cutters so that they stick out about 60 mm (2½ inches) from the cup, at their lowest point.

DID YOU KNOW?
Pachycephalosaurus had a thick, skull, like a helmet. Some scientists think they might have used it to butt heads with each other.

TURN THE HANDLE TO MAKE THEM RUN!

SCAN HERE
TO SEE US IN ACTION!

13 Thread the dinosaurs onto the wires through the holes you made earlier with a paper clip.

NODDING DIPLODOCUS

(DIP-low-DOCK-us)

This friendly dinosaur moves with the help of a swinging pendulum, using a coin for a weight. The best thing is it will always agree with you!

WHAT YOU NEED:

- Small plastic drinks bottle
- Cardboard
- Plastic lollipop stick
- Regular paper clip (about 25 mm/1 inch)
- Paper straw
- Small coin
- Assorted craft card
- White paper
- Felt-tip pens

TOOLS:

- Pair of compasses
- Pencil
- Pair of scissors
- Ruler
- Craft knife
- Strong glue
- Pair of needle-nose pliers
- Wire cutters
- School glue (PVA)

1 With a pair of compasses set to 15 mm (⅝ inch), draw a circle on each side of the bottle.

2 Cut out the two circles.

3 Draw around the lid of the bottle onto a piece of cardboard and then cut it out.

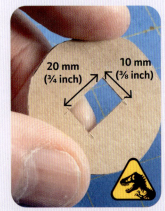

20 mm (¾ inch)   10 mm (⅜ inch)

4 Cut out a hole in the middle of the cardboard.

5 Cut two 10 mm (⅜-inch) lengths from the end of the lollipop stick. These plastic tubes will be used for the pendulum axle to run through.

You can eat your lollipop now!

6 Use strong glue to secure the tubes on each side of the rectangular hole.

7 Attach the cardboard disc to the top of the bottle with strong glue.

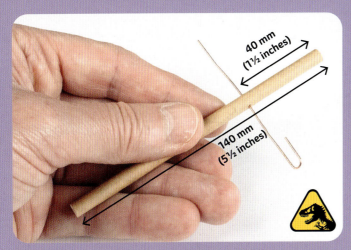

40 mm (1½ inches)

140 mm (5½ inches)

8 Cut the straw to length. Straighten a paper clip as shown, and make holes in the straw with it, 40 mm (1½ inches) from one end.

Bottom of pendulum

9 To make a pendulum, use strong glue to attach the coin to the long end of the straw.

10 Thread the pendulum into position, through the hole in the bottle, and secure it with the paper clip, as shown. Make sure it swings freely.

Fold and trim paper clips ends

11 Fold the ends of the paper clip 90 degrees with pliers so that the paper clip stays in place. Use wire cutters to trim the ends.

Glue on a paper circle for the eye.

13 Use strong glue to attach the dinosaur neck to the top of the straw. Make sure the dinosaur can swing freely.

12 Draw the outline of a Diplodocus head and neck onto craft card, then cut it out. Add markings with felt-tip pens.

14 Cut out some foliage, with slits to fit around the lollipop sticks. Fold the ends and attach them to the cardboard lid, in front of the dinosaur, with school glue.

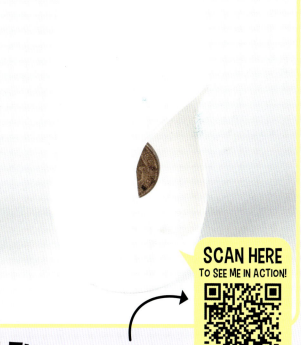

DID YOU KNOW?

Much like giraffes do today, Diplodocuses would have used their long necks to reach vegetation high up in the trees.

SCAN HERE
TO SEE ME IN ACTION!

NUDGE THE BOTTLE TO MAKE THE DIPLODOCUS SWAY ITS LONG NECK BACK AND FORTH.

Use the QR code to access the template you need.

WHAT YOU NEED:

- Thin cardboard
- Craft card
- White paper
- Felt-tip pens

TOOLS:

- Pair of scissors
- School glue (PVA)

As far as we know, all dinosaurs laid eggs. What kind of baby dinosaur will you put inside your surprise hatching egg?

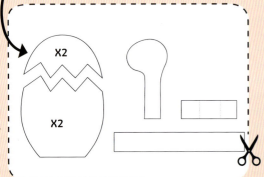

1 Copy or trace the egg pieces twice and a long tab onto thin cardboard. Then copy the dinosaur head and sleeve onto craft card. Cut them all out.

2 Glue the dinosaur head to the long tab. Wrap and glue the sleeve around the long tab, so that it slides up and down freely.

3 Add markings and features to the head, using white paper and felt-tip pens.

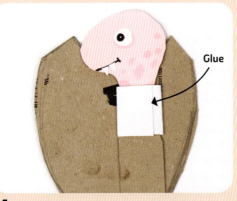

Glue

4 Glue the sleeve to the inside of the lower egg shell, so that the head can slide up and down.

5 Glue both of the upper shells onto the front and back of the head.

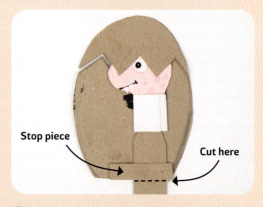

Stop piece

Cut here

6 Cut a 50 x 12 mm (2 x ½ inch) stop piece from a scrap of cardboard, and glue it to the slider, as shown, to limit how much the egg can open. Cut off the excess slider below the stop.

FRONT

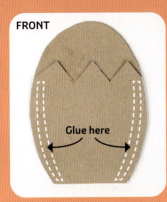

Glue here

BACK

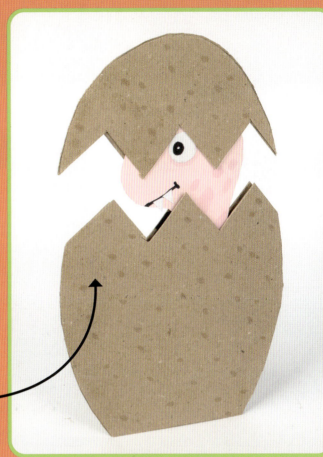

7 Glue the front of the egg into place along the sides, so that the slider can move freely.

8 Make a stand by folding a rectangle of cardboard in half and gluing it to the back of the egg.

LIFT THE TOP OF THE EGG TO HATCH THE DINOSAUR!

DID YOU KNOW?
Gigantoraptor arranged their eggs in enormous circular nests. They left the middle empty so they could sit on the nest without crushing the eggs.

SMASHING ANKYLOSAURUS

(an-KIE-loh-sore-us)

Use the QR code to access the template you need.

WHAT YOU NEED:

- Cardboard
- Felt-tip pens
- Plastic eyes
- Craft cork
- 2 jumbo paper clips (about 50 mm/2 inches)
- 6mm/ 1/4 inch glass bead
- 4mm /1/8 inch glass bead
- Plastic lollipop stick (cut to 25 mm/ 1 inch long)

TOOLS:

- Pair of scissors
- Strong glue
- Craft drill
- Pair of needle-nose pliers
- Wire cutters
- School glue (PVA)

This little Ankylosaurus model, with its swinging tail, is a real corker!

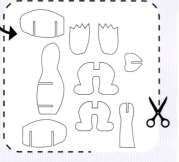

1 Copy or trace the shapes from the template onto cardboard and cut them out.

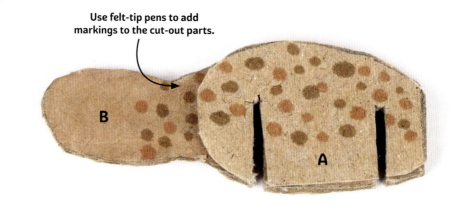

Use felt-tip pens to add markings to the cut-out parts.

B

A

2 Use school glue to join the two side pieces (A) to each side of the body (B), so that all the slits line up.

C

D

E

3 Slide the legs (C and D) into place and glue the head pieces (E) onto the body, as shown. Glue on some plastic eyes.

12 mm (¹/₂ inch)

4 Drill a hole right through the cork, 12 mm (½ inch) from one end.

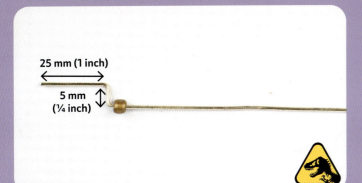

5 Straighten out a jumbo paper clip, bend it as shown, using a pair of pliers, and then thread the 4mm bead into place. This will become the crank.

25 mm (1 inch)

5 mm (¼ inch)

Bead

Lollipop tube

6 Thread the wire through the hole in the cork. Then use strong glue to attach the lollipop tube to the cork, so that it is flush against the bead and lined up with the top of the cork.

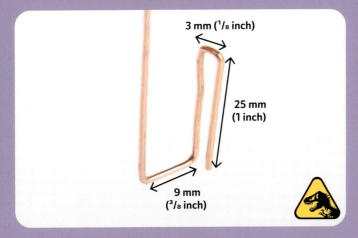

3 mm (¹/₈ inch)

25 mm (1 inch)

9 mm (³/₈ inch)

7 Straighten out the second paper clip and then bend it into shape, as shown.

Crank

8 Thread the wire up through the plastic tube and position the crank into the slot, as shown.

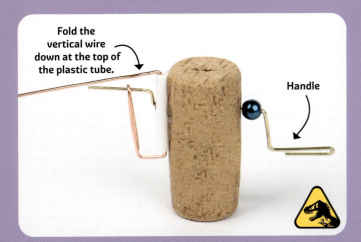

Fold the vertical wire down at the top of the plastic tube.

Handle

9 Thread the 6mm bead onto the other end of the crank, then shape the wire into a handle.

5 mm (¼ inch)

10 Fold the wire above the plastic tube and trim, as shown, using wire cutters.

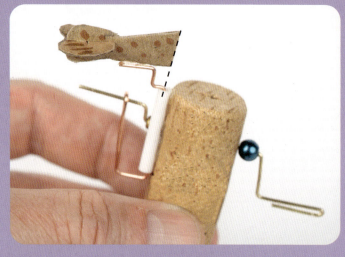

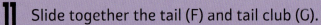

11 Slide together the tail (F) and tail club (G).

12 Glue the tail to the horizontal wire so that the top end of the tail is directly over the plastic tube.

DID YOU KNOW?

Ankylosaurus were thought to defend themselves from predators by using their heavy clublike tail.

SCAN HERE
TO SEE ME IN ACTION!

13 Complete the model by gluing the feet to the top of the cork.

WATCH THE ANKYLOSAURUS SWING ITS TAIL FROM SIDE TO SIDE!

INDEX

THE AUTHOR

Rob Ives is a UK-based designer and paper engineer. A former teacher, he now specializes in paper animations and science projects, and he often visits schools to talk about design technology and demonstrate his models. His published titles include *Paper Models That Rock!*, *Paper Automata* and the Build it! Make it! series.

PICTURE CREDITS:

(Abbreviations: t=top; b=bottom; m=middle; l=left; r=right; bg=background.

Alyona Zhitnaya (Illustrated throughout—difficulty icons); Baltazar 9090 (illustrated throughout—safety icon); Catmando 27b; Daniel Eskridge 18tl, 5tr, 12tl; Dotted Yeti 24–25b, 20–21b, 14–15b, 6bl, 28tl, 30-31b; Herschel Hoffmeger 22br, 4bg, 17b; Ldesign 7 (craft tools illustrations); NPaweIN 7m; Spreadthesign 7mr; Unununij 7br; Warpaint 22tl, 26tl, 16tl, 2bg; Winwin art lab (footprint illustration - illustrated throughout); YuRi Photolife 1ml, 8tl, 11tr, 10–11b.

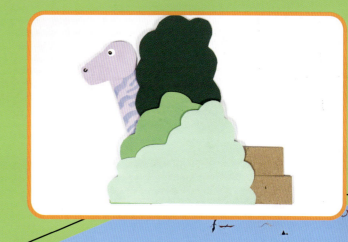